OPERATION SEA LION: A JOINT CRITICAL ANALYSIS

Lt Col Randy McCanne, USAF
LTC Greg D. Olson, USA
CDR Dario E. Teicher, USN

Joint Forces Staff College
Joint and Combined Warfighting Course
Class 02-3S
30 August 2002

Faculty Advisor:
Col Sheryl Debnam
Seminar A

Report Documentation Page		*Form Approved* *OMB No. 0704-0188*

Public reporting burden for the collection of information is estimated to average 1 hour per response, including the time for reviewing instructions, searching existing data sources, gathering and maintaining the data needed, and completing and reviewing the collection of information. Send comments regarding this burden estimate or any other aspect of this collection of information, including suggestions for reducing this burden, to Washington Headquarters Services, Directorate for Information Operations and Reports, 1215 Jefferson Davis Highway, Suite 1204, Arlington VA 22202-4302. Respondents should be aware that notwithstanding any other provision of law, no person shall be subject to a penalty for failing to comply with a collection of information if it does not display a currently valid OMB control number.

1. REPORT DATE **30 AUG 2002**	2. REPORT TYPE **N/A**	3. DATES COVERED **-**
4. TITLE AND SUBTITLE **Operation Sea Lion: A Joint Critical Analysis**		5a. CONTRACT NUMBER
		5b. GRANT NUMBER
		5c. PROGRAM ELEMENT NUMBER
6. AUTHOR(S) **Lt Col Randy McCanne, USAF; LTC Greg D. Olson, USA; CDR Dario E. Teicher, USN**		5d. PROJECT NUMBER
		5e. TASK NUMBER
		5f. WORK UNIT NUMBER
7. PERFORMING ORGANIZATION NAME(S) AND ADDRESS(ES) **Joint Forces Staff College 7800 Hampton Blvd Norfolk, VA 23511-1701**		8. PERFORMING ORGANIZATION REPORT NUMBER
9. SPONSORING/MONITORING AGENCY NAME(S) AND ADDRESS(ES)		10. SPONSOR/MONITOR'S ACRONYM(S)
		11. SPONSOR/MONITOR'S REPORT NUMBER(S)

12. DISTRIBUTION/AVAILABILITY STATEMENT
Approved for public release, distribution unlimited

13. SUPPLEMENTARY NOTES
Taken from the Internet.

14. ABSTRACT
See report.

15. SUBJECT TERMS

16. SECURITY CLASSIFICATION OF:			17. LIMITATION OF ABSTRACT	18. NUMBER OF PAGES	19a. NAME OF RESPONSIBLE PERSON
a. REPORT **unclassified**	b. ABSTRACT **unclassified**	c. THIS PAGE **unclassified**	**UU**	**28**	

Standard Form 298 (Rev. 8-98)
Prescribed by ANSI Std Z39-18

I. Introduction

Military history contains many lessons from which the warfighting doctrine of the individual services, as well as joint doctrine, is derived. World War II stands as one of the major contributors of valuable lessons learned. From a joint and combined warfighting perspective, Germany's planning and preparatory military actions to the invasion of Great Britain after the fall of France are instructive. Their plan, called Operation SEA LION by the Germans, was never carried out, as certain prerequisite conditions were never achieved, and Hitler elected to move on to other operations. But Germany could have been successful in invading and, if necessary, occupying Great Britain had they exercised joint and combined operations to achieve better unity of effort within the German military, remained focused on key British operational centers of gravity, and exploited the capabilities of friendly nations such as Spain, Italy, and the Vichy government of France.

II. Background

A. Political Situation

World War II began with the German invasion of Poland on 1 September 1939. The German dictator, Adolf Hitler, advised his armed forces in *Fuehrer Directive No. 1:* "All political means having been exhausted to correct in a peaceful manner the unbearable situation on Germany's eastern border, I have decided upon a solution by force" (9, 49).

The "unbearable situation" was the separation of East Prussia from Germany by the creation of Poland following World War I. Cleverly, Hitler had isolated Poland through "political means" and shaped the battlefield in his favor. He secured Germany's eastern borders when on 23 August 1939 Germany signed a nonaggression pact with the Soviet Union in which both secretly agreed to dismember Poland (21). Great Britain and France had offered Poland defense guarantees, and both declared war on Germany two days after the invasion; but with the Soviet Union in the German camp, the guarantees proved worthless. Trapped between Germany and the Soviet Union, a surrounded Poland ceased to exist in less than one month.

Meanwhile, to the south, Hitler had forged a close alliance with fellow Fascist dictator Benito Mussolini of Italy. In 1936, Italy had entered into a formal alliance with Germany known as the Rome-Berlin Axis. The Axis would later include Japan in September 1940 (2). Overseas in the United States, isolationist sentiments were strong, and in any case France and Britain appeared to have the balance of power in their favor. Hence, Americans hoped to remain on the sidelines and out of the trenches of yet another European war (1, 55).

However, on 10 May 1940, the Germans invaded the West, and by 19 June the German High Command of the Armed Forces (*Ober Kommando der Wehrmacht*) announced, "The Fuehrer intends to stage a big parade in Paris" (9, 104). Three days later, after a short 43-day campaign, France surrendered and the Germans paraded under the *Arc de Triomphe* (1, 5). The redistribution of power on the European continent meant those minor powers not yet conquered by Germany, such as Switzerland and Hungary, were quickly cowed into pro-German neutrality or aligned with the Axis powers (2). Across the English Channel, Great Britain stood alone refusing to yield to German peace overtures and clinging to the hope that America would awaken from its isolationist stupor (1, 5).

B. Military Situation

In the summer of 1940, Germany became the hegemon of Europe. The rapid defeat of Poland showed the world a new combat doctrine called *blitzkrieg* (lightning-war) that combined the effects of infantry, armor, and aircraft in a massive display of firepower and mobility. All doubts regarding mechanized warfare were eliminated when Germany defeated France. "On the evening of 20 May, (German General) Guderian's panzer divisions reached the Channel coast at the mouth of the Somme. The French northern armies and the BEF (British Expeditionary Forces) had been cut off" (17, 23). The campaign continued into June, but the outcome was already decided in the first ten days. France, the best-equipped army in the world, had fallen victim to blitzkrieg, and the BEF had to flee by sea abandoning all its equipment on the beaches of Dunkirk (1, 15).

The brilliance of the operational and tactical plans to defeat France was not fully appreciated or anticipated by Germany's strategic commanders. No plan existed to follow up a decisive victory. Even after the panzers reached the English Channel, no serious consideration was given to the need for a campaign plan that called for the invasion of England. For example, the Germans needed ships, yet in the euphoria of victory they made no demands regarding the disposition of the powerful French fleet in the surrender terms, nor were there considerations to seize any of these naval units (1, 106). The German Commander in Chief of the Navy (Kriegsmarine), Admiral Raeder, recalled after the war, "Our mental as well as materiel preparations before the war had not been aimed at an armed conflict with England" (17, 82). Therefore, Hitler hoped the rapid defeat of France would be enough to encourage Britain to agree to peace terms.

By July 1940 it was apparent that Britain had no intentions of surrendering. Indeed, Prime Minister Churchill, in reference to a possible German invasion, had declared, "If the long history of our island is to come to an end, then it shall only end when every last one of us is beaten to the ground and lies choking in his blood" (17, 70). In the face of British stubbornness, the Ober Kommando der Wehrmacht (OKW) on 2 July 1940 issued orders to commence planning Operation SEA LION; the cross-channel amphibious assault on the beaches of England (9, 105).

III. Centers of Gravity

"The first task, then, in planning for war is to identify the enemy's centers of gravity, and if possible trace them back to a single one."

Carl von Clausewitz

A. Centers of Gravity Defined

According to Joint Publication 1, *Joint Warfare of the Armed Forces of the United States,* knowledge of the enemy is one of the fundamentals of joint warfare (12, III-13). Success in warfare depends on understanding the adversary's critical vulnerabilities, capabilities, limitations, centers of gravity, and potential courses of action. Without such knowledge, or with only an incomplete understanding of these aspects of the enemy, the probability of success is diminished. Of these characteristics, perhaps the most important to the success of a campaign or invasion plan is to understand the enemy's centers of gravity.

Centers of gravity (COGs) ought to be the focus of campaign planning at both the strategic and operational levels. Clausewitz described COGs in the military context as "the hub of all power and movement, on which everything depends." Joint doctrine defines COGs as "Those characteristics, capabilities, or localities from which a military force derives its freedom of action, physical strength, or will to fight" (12, III-13). Therefore, improper COG analysis can lead to expending limited military forces against enemy targets of little importance to the final outcome. Attacking COGs means concentrating against capabilities whose destruction or overthrow is most likely to yield success with the minimum of effort.

B. Enemy Centers of Gravity

An analysis of Hitler's *Fuehrer Directive No. 16*, which directed the General Staff and the service commanders in chief to begin planning Operation SEA LION, quickly reveals the British operational centers of gravity. The directive defined a number of prerequisites that the Kriegsmarine and Luftwaffe had to achieve before a cross-channel invasion could be attempted

  a. The British air force must be subdued….
  b. Mine-free passages are to be created.
  c. The Strait of Dover, as well as the western entrance of the Channel is to be tightly sealed off with minefields…
  d. The coast is to be dominated and sealed off by…coastal artillery.
  e. It is desirable to tie down the British naval forces…in the North Sea as well as in the Mediterranean (the latter by the Italians)…. (9, 108)

Effectively, according to *Directive 16,* for Operation SEA LION to succeed the mighty Royal Navy had to be deterred and the full strength of a Royal Air Force had to be defeated for the Germans to be able to support ground operations across the English Channel. *Directive 16* hardly mentions the British Army, perhaps because it was severely degraded during the evacuation from Dunkirk and posed no immediate threat. But it is clear that a German invasion would have to deal with what was left of the British ground forces upon landing, and they should thus be considered a center of gravity. Ultimately, all would rest on who commanded the air and sea on both sides of the English Channel; thus, the RAF and Royal Navy would be the two centers of gravity posing the biggest challenge.

C. The British Army

Even though some 215,000 British troops escaped in the near-miracle of the Dunkirk evacuation, much of their equipment, particularly the heavy weaponry, was necessarily left behind (3, 121). The British Army desperately needed time—time to reorganize, reequip, and prepare defensive positions.

Hitler missed a golden opportunity at Dunkirk to largely destroy the BEF. On 24 May 1940, German General Guderian's Panzers were within 15 miles of Dunkirk while four motorized divisions and at least six infantry divisions were closing in as well. Dunkirk, and with it more than

300,000 British and French troops, was "ripe for the taking" when the panzers were ordered to halt and stand fast (3, 55).

If Hitler had recognized the British Army as a COG for the invasion of England, perhaps he would have done more to prevent their evacuation from Dunkirk. In consequence, Operation SEA LION called for a much larger invasion force than might otherwise have been necessary, further complicating invasion plans and endangering chances of success.

D. The Royal Navy

While the British Army was in disarray after the evacuation from Dunkirk, the Royal Navy outmatched German naval forces. The Kriegsmarine lost nearly half its surface fleet during the invasion of Norway in April 1940 and would have to rely heavily upon the Luftwaffe to turn any major naval engagement in Germany's favor (23, 111).

In addition to the Luftwaffe, Hitler and his staff were forced to place a lot of faith in coastal artillery (8, 32) and maritime minefields (8, 45) as "antidotes" to the Royal Navy. Ultimately, it was not a reassessment of the naval risks but the failure to establish air supremacy that made Hitler call off the invasion. All the evidence suggests that, had Germany won the air battle, Hitler's armies would have embarked and sailed according to plan. (8, 150)

E. The Royal Air Force

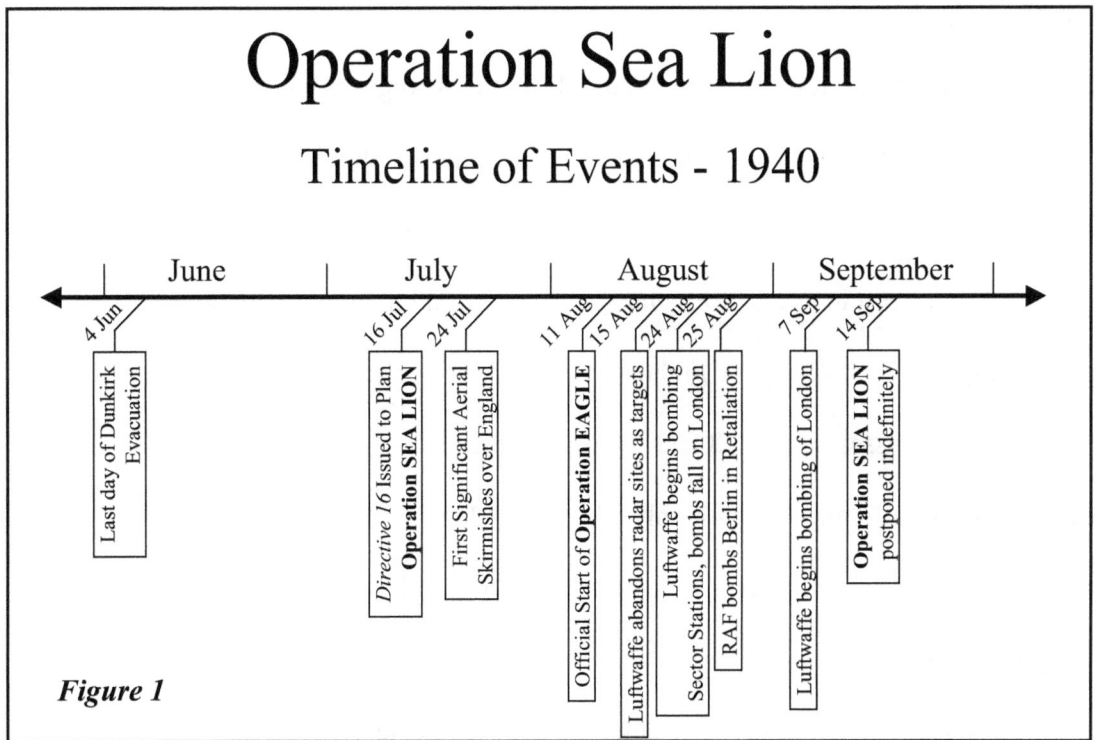

Figure 1

The most important center of gravity and hence the British "hub of all power and movement" was the RAF. For an invasion to be successful, German strategy required air supremacy and not simply superiority in the air over southern England, the Channel, and the Continental ports from which the invasion was to be launched (8, 235). Perhaps more than any other aspect of the period, from Dunkirk to the end of the summer, German air strategy reflects the flaws in their understanding of this center of gravity (8, 213). In particular, German failure to press successful strategies for degrading RAF radar, command and control, and other critical air defense systems indicates impatience in dealing with this key COG.

Figure 1 above shows significant events in the Battle of Britain (Operation EAGLE) and reinforces the view that Germany did not remain focused on any one set of targets long enough to effectively suppress the objective and achieve the operational task. The result was the indefinite postponement of Operation SEA LION.

Operation EAGLE focused initially on three tasks until 24 August 1940 as follows:

1) The main effort was to overwhelm the frontline of British air defenses in southern England by drawing Fighter Command into battle and eliminating it through attrition. The RAF had the upper hand, at least in terms of loss ratios, because of a remarkably effective early warning and C2 system that often gave Fighter Command the initiative when engaging the enemy. Even so, British losses between 8 and 18 August included 154 pilots, with only 63 new pilots accessioned, and 213 aircraft, with only 150 replaced (8, 234). Evidence suggests that if Germany had kept up the pressure long enough, the RAF would have been forced to disengage from the fight or be destroyed.

2) As a supporting effort, the plan called for probing the left (northeast) flank of the island. Luftwaffe forces operating from Scandinavia were ordered to bomb targets in northeast England on 15 August 1940. The German bombers, escorted by long-range but inferior ME-110 fighters, were intercepted well out to sea and the force suffered losses so great that Germany never again attempted daylight operations over England from that approach (8, 228). England's left flank was found to be adequately defended.

3) Finally, the plan required the bombing of aircraft production factories (8, 233). An important feature of the German air war plan was night attacks against aircraft plants. Daylight raids tended to suffer greater losses. The poor level of accuracy of the night bombing generally hampered the effectiveness of such attacks. Even so, the Germans were right to attack those targets but wrong to defer the attacks to the last moment (8, 227). If attacks against those targets

had begun shortly after the fall of France, the effects would have been much more significant and possibly hadn an impact on the final outcome.

On 12 August 1940, the Germans attacked and damaged five radar stations, one of which was not put back into operation for 11 days (8, 223). This was a significant achievement and would have been even more so if the Germans had continued to attack this set of targets. However, German commanders did not know "the role that radar played in the system.... It was assumed that Fighter Command fought a decentralized battle, with squadrons tied to the radio range of their individual stations, attacks on radar were not given high enough priority" (20, 79). Just three days after their successful attack the Luftwaffe largely abandoned radar targets.

After 24 August, the Luftwaffe began attacks on the sector stations, which performed an important command and control function for Fighter Command: group HQ launched the squadrons based on early warning information, then the sector stations passed by radio the latest combat intelligence from radar and forward observers, guiding the pilots into battle on advantageous terms (8, 233). By 6 September 1940, severe and cumulative damage to the sector stations was having a clear impact on the effectiveness of the RAF in repelling air attacks. The Luftwaffe was achieving the most favorable loss ratios of the war. Churchill wrote afterwards, "The scales had tilted against Fighter Command" (8, 236).

On 24 August 1940, the Germans made a fateful mistake that changed the course of the battle. German bombers with orders to attack British aircraft factories and oil installations on the extreme perimeter of London missed their mark and instead the bombs fell on residential districts in northern and eastern London, resulting in heavy casualties and leaving many Londoners homeless. Churchill subsequently ordered the bombing of Berlin on the following night. That bombing caused little real damage, but Hitler had often implied to his people that no bombs would ever fall on Berlin. Hitler lost face and promised devastating reprisals, which began on 7 September 1940. This switch in priorities undoubtedly saved Fighter Command (8, 276-278).

In retrospect, the factors that undermined the effectiveness of the German air campaign were largely self-inflicted. Many of the targets attacked were of secondary importance, and no target set, "whether airfields, communications, ports or industry, was attacked repeatedly, systematically, or accurately" (20, 115). Failure of the Luftwaffe to press attacks against these targets allowed the RAF to recover and continue the fight.

IV. Unity of Effort

According to the *Doctrine for Joint Operations*, "unity of effort…requires coordination and cooperation among all forces toward a commonly recognized objective" (13, A-2). Following the defeat of France, instead of unity, the Wehrmacht found themselves in confusion without a plan to prosecute the war against Great Britain. In fact, the High Command of the Army (OKH), the Luftwaffe, and Kriegsmarine believed the war was over. For example, "OKH actually began to send 40 divisions home, because it did not know what to do…. (The service commanders)…were unable to imagine that the Fuhrer did not have a clearly defined objective" (17, 92).

In the confusion, the Germans failed in at least three joint planning facets that made Operation SEA LION an impossible mission. First, *unity of command* had to be maintained to properly focus German military power on its last remaining enemy. Also, a new *commander's intent* had to be announced to the armed forces in view of the unanticipated early fall of France. Consequently, a new *concept of operations* had to be drafted to achieve the revised end-state.

A. Unity of Command

During the Second World War, Hitler was both the political and military leader of Germany. He often blurred the strategic, operational, and even tactical levels of command, usually becoming involved in all aspects of a military campaign. He forced unity of effort using OKW to coordinate the Army, Kriegsmarine and Luftwaffe, providing them strategic and operational direction. The German military was not a well-oiled joint system, and Hitler's involvement was usually necessary to overcome service rivalries (18, 51).

Throughout the war, there was friction between OKW, OKH, and the Luftwaffe. This was due to the establishment of OKW to oversee the service branches and the creation of the Luftwaffe, which was led by the politically powerful Reich Marshal Goring. Both deprived OKH of its previously elevated position. In earlier wars, OKH had been predominant with the Kriegsmarine as a supporting command. The revised organization had the three branches under OKW and OKW under Hitler (18, 58).

Normally, Hitler was able to create unity among the three service branches by becoming personally involved. This was not the case for SEA LION. He allowed the three branches to flounder in interservice squabbles and seldom interfered. Without Hitler's involvement, OKW did not have sufficient stature to force unity of effort among the services. Instead, decisions regarding SEA LION became the product of compromise and not necessarily the best solutions (17, 265).

Furthermore, *Directive 16* did not attempt to compensate for Hitler's lack of involvement by designating an overall SEA LION commander, thus establishing unity of command and perhaps leading to unity of effort. Instead, *Directive 16* embedded interservice confusion by ordering "each (Service) Commander in Chief will lead those belonging to his particular branch, under my orders and according to my general directives" (9, 108). However, as already stated, Hitler remained aloof; without him there was no unity of command, and the concept of operations for SEA LION began to suffer. One is left to agree with Kieser, who writes in *Hitler on the Door-*

step, "Left to themselves, the three commanders in chief would certainly never have reached agreement, only a Fuhrer order could have forced them to do so" (17, 265).

B. The Commander's Intent

The unexpected rapid demise of France and Britain's refusal to yield forced Hitler to revise his "commander's intent." According to the *Doctrine for Joint Operations*: "The commander's intent describes the desired end-state. It is a concise expression of the purpose of the operation…. (The commander's intent) is the initial impetus for the entire planning process" (13, III-26).

Initially, the German intent was to subdue Britain through slow, "long term economic warfare…using the Luftwaffe and Kriegsmarine to cut her supply lines" (7, 218). No serious consideration was given to an amphibious assault on the English coast, and the end-state against Britain was nebulous. In fact, immediately following the defeat of France, Hitler's desired end-state "was for [Britain] to acknowledge Germany's position on the Continent [and]…to make peace…on a basis that…[Britain] would regard as compatible with her honor to accept" (7, 218). Under that end-state, it was up to Britain to decide whether or not economic warfare and generous peace overtures would make her succumb and thus bring the war to an end.

Perhaps aware of this dilemma and following Britain's rejection of several peace overtures, Hitler at last proposed to force a decision by taking advantage of the apparent window of opportunity caused by the fall of France and the disorganized hasty retreat of the BEF. On 16 July 1940, he finally provided the "impetus" for Operation SEA LION issuing *Directive No. 16,* in which he redefined the end-state, calling for the occupation of English soil "to eliminate the British homeland as a base for continuing the war against Germany" (9, 107). Arguably, the window of opportunity was rapidly closing, but Operation SEA LION required slow meticulous planning because an opposed amphibious operation was a novel concept for the German military and the required resources had to be gathered.

The British high command including Prime Minister Churchill was certain the Germans would cross immediately after the French surrender and doubted a successful beachhead could be prevented. They did not expect an opportunity to rearm the BEF to provide adequate force-on-force opposition. Instead, it was the British intent to make the German breakout from the beaches costly by conducting conventional operations when possible and guerilla warfare always (17, 263). It was best expressed by Churchill on 4 June 1940 before the House of Commons when he said, "We shall fight on the beaches, we shall fight on the landing grounds, we shall fight in the fields and in the streets, we shall fight in the hills; we shall never surrender" (5). Consequently, with all their equipment lost in France, poorly armed British troops awaited throughout 1940 what initially appeared to be certain invasion.

C. Concept of Operations

The British and Germans recalled that on 9 April 1940, with airborne troops in the vanguard, a German ground force had been successfully transported by sea to conquer Norway (17, 29). The Royal Navy was initially surprised but eventually punished the smaller Kriegsmarine. The German surface fleet lost nearly half its strength in vessels sunk or seriously damaged, but accomplished its mission of delivering troops into poorly defended Norwegian harbors; no beach assaults were conducted. Ultimately, lack of adequate Norwegian defenses and the unchallenged powerful Luftwaffe decided the battle in Germany's favor (23, 111).

The lesson drawn by both the British and Germans was that amphibious operations were possible when under an air force umbrella and despite a weak navy (10, 27). In addition, the Kriegsmarine's after-action reports indicate that in the Norwegian campaign there was "smooth cooperation between the three services" (10, 26). That was one lesson the Germans did not incorporate as they prepared for SEA LION.

Notwithstanding the poor materiel condition of the British Army, the Germans faced a much tougher task in Operation SEA LION. Without amphibious assault experience, the planning resembled a large river crossing. In fact, 1,910 river barges to be towed by 419 tugs were gathered in preparation to ferry troops to the beaches. The plan envisioned soldiers moving from the barges into fast riverine assault craft for the initial assault wave. Later waves would have the barges move heavy equipment directly onto the beach, although the hope was for the early capture of a functioning port. Airborne troops would be employed for this task and once again be the vanguard of the invasion force. Above all, the crossing was dependent on calm weather. The flat bottoms of the barges would be swamped and risk sinking in anything beyond sea state 3. Furthermore, the Germans knew that unlike Norway, England would thoroughly oppose this undertaking (19, 155).

Despite Norway, Hitler appeared to have "no stomach for amphibious operations" (19, 159). He allowed dubious compromises to be made between the service branches. For example, in order to deter the Royal Navy, the Kriegsmarine proposed landings on a narrow front. This would allow better concentration of their submarines, torpedo boats, and defensive mine fields to guard the flanks of the ground assault waves, crossing from Calais to Dover (the shortest distance), against the expected Royal Navy onslaught. On the contrary, the German Army preferred to assault on a broad front (the whole length of the English southern coast) to avoid giving the British the opportunity to contain a narrow beachhead (17, 92).

The German Army was concerned that the 200.000-man BEF that had escaped from Dunkirk and possibly additional ground forces from Britain's vast empire would bottle up the beachhead.

However, the Kriegsmarine knew the Royal Navy would sortie into the channel and, if not properly defended, the length of the beachfront would be purely academic. The debate raged with Hitler vacillating, and instead of a best decision, he allowed an uncomfortable compromise (17, 93). The initial landings would take place between Bognor and Ramsgate on the coast of England, east of the Isle of Wight; half of the beachfront desired by the Army and probably more than the Kriegsmarine could protect (7, 221).

The one issue where there was absolute agreement among the branches of the Wehrmacht was in the air. The Luftwaffe had to achieve command of the air to then be able to concentrate against the Royal Navy's attempts to interfere with the crossing of troops and supplies. Otherwise, a successful German landing would eventually wither through British interdiction of the sea lines of communication leading to the beachheads (17, 86).

Elstein in "Operation SEA LION: The Plan to Invade England," argues "that SEA LION was impossible without air supremacy, and superfluous if air supremacy were achieved" (7, 220). The statement is simplistic, but the British in 1940 seem to have echoed his sentiments. According to the British Admiralty, to oppose SEA LION, "the action of the navy's light forces (patrol boats, destroyers, and some cruisers) against enemy transports would be limited to the range of air cover provided by Fighter Command." The battleships and heavy cruisers would remain out of the range of German aircraft, 24 hours away in northern ports, until the actual beach assault had commenced. (19, 148). Clearly, the British too understood that it all depended on who commanded the air.

Therefore, one can argue that in fact Operation SEA LION was launched on 13 August 1940. The first phase was the Luftwaffe's effort to achieve air supremacy over England, Operation EAGLE.

On 1 August 1940, *Fuehrer Directive No. 17* ordered, "The Luftwaffe is to overcome the British Air Force with all means at its disposal and in the shortest possible time. The attacks are to be directed primarily against the planes themselves, their ground installations, and their supply organizations, also against aircraft industry" (9, 110).

By 6 September 1940, British Fighter Command was close to the breaking point. During the previous two weeks, Fighter Command had suffered 295 fighters destroyed and 171 seriously damaged with only 269 new aircraft produced. Also, 300 pilots had been lost and only 260 replacement pilots generated by the flying schools. Air Chief Marshal Dowding of Fighter Command was on the verge of withdrawing the remainder of his forces to northern England to be re-committed when the actual amphibious landings occurred. In fact, the British Armed Forces were placed on highest alert in early September 1940 believing command of the air was about to be lost and the invasion was imminent (19, 150).

Suddenly, the situation changed when an insignificant British bombing raid on Berlin led Hitler to lose sight of the objective (the defeat of the RAF) (19, 153). He ordered at this crucial moment retaliatory air strikes against London. "From 7 September 1940, London was bombed for a total of fifty-seven consecutive nights" (22). The London Blitz had won a reprieve for Fighter Command. The people of London suffered, but Operation EAGLE failed and with it any hope for Operation SEA LION.

V. Friendly Nations

In August 1939, as Germany prepared for war, Hitler clearly understood the need for allies and friendly governments to secure the German position in the coming war. Defining the German geopolitical position to his commanders in chief, he said:

> There are many factors in our favor at present and they may not last.... Probably

no one will ever again have the confidence of the whole German people, as I do.... Mussolini's existence is also vital. If something happens to him, Italy's loyalty will be no longer certain.... A third personal factor favorable to us is Franco. We can only ask benevolent neutrality from Spain. But even that depends on Franco's personality. All these fortunate circumstances will no longer prevail in two or three years. No one knows how long I shall live.... We have no choice; we must act.... Therefore conflict is better now.... (11, 24)

This positive state of affairs was even more in favor of Germany upon the conclusion of the dramatically successful campaign in France. This event coupled to the Nazi-Soviet Non-Aggression Pact, which had secured Germany's eastern borders, shifted the military balance of power decisively in Germany's favor vis-à-vis Great Britain.

Although Britain stood alone in the summer of 1940, it still held a superior geostrategic position anchored by a vast empire defended by a powerful navy and strong air force. In preparation for SEA LION, Germany toyed with the notion of using allies to challenge the Royal Navy and perhaps sever British lines of communication within the empire. For example, *Directive 16* mentions the use of the Italian fleet to fix British naval forces in the Mediterranean to facilitate the SEA LION crossing.

In the end, Germany's allies were not part of the SEA LION planning process. In fact, there was very little coordination between the Axis powers. For example, Italy invaded Greece, disrupting German plans against Russia; Spain stonewalled German invitations to enter the war; and Japan never opened a second front against Russia and attacked the United States without consulting its Axis partners (16, 131).

According to the *Doctrine for Planning Joint Operations,* "an alliance is the result of formal agreements (i.e., treaties) between two or more nations for broad, long-term objectives that further the common interests of the members" (14, II-21). The Axis nations had signed the agreement, but the extent of their common interest was limited. One must wonder if a combined Axis campaign plan against Britain might have perhaps identified British vulnerabilities that would have contributed towards a successful Operation SEA LION.

A. Italy

Shortly before the fall of France, Italy entered World War II, opening possibilities in the Mediterranean for the Axis powers. Although comparatively weak, Italy could have contributed to the success of Operation SEA LION, but the Germans and Italians had to engage in early consultation, establish a common policy, and generate combined plans. However, German efforts to assist Italy in overcoming its material weakness and poor staff work were "frustrated by Mussolini's reluctance to accept help" (16, 149). Hitler blamed the Italians for being "jealous and childish" (16, 149).

Perhaps plans should have been in place for an Axis offensive along the Mediterranean periphery to support German operations against Great Britain following the defeat of France. The Central Mediterranean position of Italy and its modern navy were a threat to the nearby British Island of Malta, a key base on the British Mediterranean sea line of communication (SLOC.) The early fall of Malta would have severed this vital SLOC, forcing the British to rely solely on the much longer SLOC around South Africa for resources coming from her Middle Eastern and Asian colonies. Also, the Italian SLOC to its colony in Libya would have been secured (11, 99).

Furthermore, early on, the Germans should have identified the Suez Canal as the gateway to the British East African, Middle Eastern, and Far Eastern colonies and therefore a vital objective to unhinge British economic power. Hence, the Germans could have combined with Italy in the failed Italian offensive into Egypt of September 1940 and probably changed that outcome. One should recall that in February 1941, after the threat of SEA LION, the Germans belatedly introduced two armored divisions (the fabled Afrika Korps) to reinforce the much-weakened Italians in Libya and almost won in the Western Desert. An earlier arrival, while SEA LION was still a threat, and Britain would have been on the horns of a dilemma considering the risk of reinforcing Egypt with the imminent threat of Operation SEA LION (16, 149).

B. Spain

Hitler identified the Rock of Gibraltar as an important objective in Germany's war against Britain, but he waited until after the cancellation of SEA LION to approach Spain to discuss the possibility of a combined attack against the British fortress. On 23 October 1940, he met with the Spanish Fascist dictator, General Francisco Franco, to discuss terms for Spanish belligerency against Britain. Franco declared himself ready under the following conditions: that the Axis powers reward him with Gibraltar, French Morocco, and Western Algeria; and make available military and economic aid, particularly petroleum and wheat (4). Hitler agreed but was concerned about committing French colonial interests to the Spanish camp, not wanting to upset the Vichy French. He hoped to persuade the Vichy government by promising it parts of British West Africa. Ultimately, Spain continued to drag its heels and never served as a base against Gibraltar, but did contribute "volunteer" ground forces to the German Eastern Front (16, 131).

If Spain had been part of an overall campaign plan against Britain, then perhaps early in 1940, and almost certainly following the euphoric victory over France, Germany could have at least won access to Spain for an assault on Gibraltar. A successful seizure of Gibraltar would have made the Mediterranean an Axis lake protecting the Axis from enemy incursions into Europe from that direction. Simultaneously, Gibraltar's fall would have allowed the numerically significant Italian fleet to sail to French Channel ports and be available for Operation SEA LION (16, 131).

C. Vichy France

The government of France had moved to the town of Vichy as part of the armistice agreement reached with Germany following the French military's defeat. Also, the Vichy government still exercised control over the many French colonies and the French Navy. Surprisingly, during the invasion of France, the Germans never tried to forcibly seize any of the French naval units. Instead, the bulk of the French fleet sailed to ports in the French colonies of North Africa. Furthermore, Article 8 of the armistice with Germany confirmed lack of German foresight regarding the need for reflagged French warships for an invasion of England. Article 8 promised, "The German government solemnly undertook to refrain from using the French fleet for its own purposes" (6, 206).

Churchill was not ready to trust the defeated French and German guarantees. On 1 July 1940, he ordered Operation CATAPULT, in which the Royal Navy was to seek and destroy the French fleet. By 1800 on that same afternoon, British warships opened fire on French ships moored in the Algerian ports of Oran and Mers El Kebir. Despite the British effort, a heavy cruiser, six cruisers, a seaplane carrier, and five destroyers escaped safely and returned to Toulon, France (6, 207).

Following this outrageous act and with the planning for SEA LION about to commence, Hitler should have engaged Marshal Petain, leader of Vichy France, to explore the possibility of using these ships against Britain, or perhaps he should have used force to capture the vessels in Toulon. He took neither action. It was not until 24 October 1940, one month after the indefinite postponement of SEA LION, that Hitler met Petain to discuss matters of "common interest" that would possibly lead to Vichy participation in the war on the German side (16, 131).

VI. Conclusions

Three days after he ranted to an audience of thousands "I am coming! I am coming!" Hitler concentrated his air offensive on the city of London, saving the Royal Air Force from mortal attrition and undermining German air strategy (8, 132). Hitler would never again seriously contemplate an invasion. What caused Germany to abandon its plans to invade? As is shown in the preceding analysis, Operation SEA LION failed before it even started due to Germany's inability to achieve unity of effort, failure to remain focused on key operational centers of gravity, and unwillingness to exploit the capabilities of friendly nations.

A. Failure to Achieve Unity of Effort

Despite the brilliance of Blitzkrieg warfare, as already discussed, the German military had serious shortcomings regarding joint operations. *Directive 16* indicates that independent service planning was doctrinal, and it was up to Hitler through OKW to bring the three services into compliance regarding a common plan. However, when Hitler chose to avoid the planning process as he did for SEA LION, OKW did not have the power to force unity. Therefore, it appears that no one was jointly planning the war long-term, but instead the services did so crisis to crisis.

In fact, one sees that SEA LION was crisis action planning due to a shortsighted desired end-state against Britain. While Germany forced a decision through force of arms on France, Hitler based his end-state against Britain on the "hope" that Britain would sue for peace. This may be why he allowed the BEF to escape from France. No one had the foresight to see in the BEF an obstacle to a future invasion of Britain because at that instant none was planned. Thus, when the British chose to continue the war, the Wehrmacht was unprepared for amphibious operations, yet was tasked to carry them out.

B. Lost Focus on the Center of Gravity

Germany's approach to attacking the British centers of gravity suffered from both indecision and impatience. It may never be known if a more concerted effort to destroy the BEF at Dunkirk, or Germany's plans to deter the Royal Navy using coastal artillery, maritime minefields, and air power would have led to a successful invasion. But the risks posed by the British Army and Navy, while significant, paled in comparison to those posed by the Royal Air Force, and Germany's failure to defeat that COG and achieve air supremacy forced Hitler to call off the operation.

In this regard, evidence suggests that Germany correctly identified the RAF as the most critical COG, and in fact identified and attacked many of the operational centers of gravity that could have led to the defeat of the RAF, including the aircraft factories, radar and sector stations, and other supporting infrastructure that sustained or supported the RAF's warfighting capability. But bombing of aircraft production plants and support installations should have begun much earlier to have a significant impact during the planned invasion; and bombing of the radar stations, sector stations and other operational COGs that were crucial to day-to-day employment of the RAF was not sustained long enough to effectively degrade those systems. As a result, the RAF was able to recover from the attacks, continue the fight, and eventually win the Battle of Britain.

C. Failure to Include Allies

When Italy entered the war, Mediterranean opportunities became available to the Axis powers, but their failure to achieve unity of effort led to eventual defeat in the Western Desert without ever affecting Operation EAGLE or planning for Operation SEA LION. In addition, the German geopolitical position was undermined by Hitler's failure to engage friendly nations early enough to exploit their assets such as naval units or to gain geostrategic advantage through acquisition of bases against the British in preparation for Operation SEA LION.

Hitler approached both Spain and Vichy France in October 1940, but SEA LION had already been "indefinitely postponed" in September. Clearly, he missed more opportune moments to broach the topic of Spain's and Vichy's active collaboration in the war effort against Britain. For example, after the defeat of France and before Operation EAGLE, Hitler should have discussed Spanish entry into the war. Clearly, German political capital was at its highest immediately following the brilliant victory over the French. Also, in the case of the Vichy government, Hitler should have encouraged Vichy belligerency against Britain immediately following the British Operation CATAPULT of July 1940. Belatedly, by the end of October 1940, when Hitler decided to find additional allies, he had to meet with them knowing that Britain remained unconquered and had withstood the mighty Luftwaffe's best effort. Consequently, nations considering joining the Axis may have concluded that a German victory was no longer inevitable.

D. A Winning Concept of Operations

In summary, one must respond directly to the question of whether Germany could have succeeded in Operation SEA LION. The answer is yes, although a few key outcomes within the capabilities of the Wehrmacht and Hitler had to be performed differently to guarantee the greatest possibility of success.

First, once Hitler had redefined the end-state, then OKW and the service CINCs should have proceeded to plan SEA LION from a tactical, operational, and strategic perspective. The evidence discussed previously indicates that thorough strategic planning was not conducted for SEA LION. The Germans conducted their military operations oblivious to the possibility of including other friendly nations such as Italy in their war plans. They should have supported and coordinated operations with the Italians to encourage the possibility of stretching British military resources by engaging in a simultaneous offensive in the Mediterranean to support Operation EAGLE and later Operation SEA LION. The British were able through the summer of 1940 to concentrate the bulk of their armed forces in homeland defense without fearing a threat to their economic resources across the Suez Canal and beyond.

Furthermore, the Germans started World War II with an insignificant Navy, and it became even more so following their losses in the conquest of Norway. However, the strategic outlines of SEA LION never included possibilities of other countries providing naval forces. For example, an operation through Fascist Spain to seize Gibraltar, thus opening the Atlantic to the significant Italian Navy, was well within the realm of possibilities. Also, opportunities were missed to capture French warships following their surrender and certainly after the British attack on the French fleet. These warships would have been available to defend against the Royal Navy and for vital sea escort missions of supplies and troops to the beachheads.

If the end-state had initially been to occupy England, then an operational objective of the Wehrmacht would have been to capture the BEF. Instead, these troops escaped to fight another day. The existence of the under-equipped BEF defending the British beaches was enough to complicate planning. Without the BEF, German landings could have safely occurred on a narrow front. The Kriegsmarine could then adequately defend and support it against the Royal Navy.

Ultimately, Operation SEA LION was lost over the skies of England. The British center of gravity was clearly the RAF, and a sustained air campaign against aircraft factories, radar and sector stations, airfields, and other support facilities could have led to the defeat of Fighter Command and paved the way for a German invasion from the sea. As it was, German numerical superiority was such that by mid-September 1940 command of the air was within grasp. Had Hitler and the Luftwaffe remained focused on these targets instead of redirecting the effort to a militarily insignificant terror bombing of London, the outcome of the Battle of Britain, and consequently also Operation SEA LION, might well have been very different.

Bibliography

1. Agar, Herbert, *The Darkest Year: Britain Alone (June 1940 – June 1941),* New York: Doubleday & Company, Inc., 1973

2. "Axis Powers," On-line. Internet, 27 July 2002, Available from: Encarta, http://encarta.msn.com/index/conciseindex/5D/05D60000.htm?z=1&pg=2&br=1

3. Barker, A.J., *Dunkirk: The Great Escape,* New York: David McKay Company, Inc., 1977

4. Burdick, Charles B, *Germany's Military Strategy and Spain in World War II,* New York: Syracuse University Press, 1968

5. Churchill, Winston, "We Shall Fight on the Beaches," On-line. Internet, 3 August 2002, Available from: The Winston Churchill Web Page, The Churchill Center, www.winstonchurchill.org/speeches.htm

6. Elstein, David, "Operation SEA LION: The Plan to Invade England," *History of the Second World War,* Ed. Pitt, Barrie, Marshall Cavendish Corp., 1978

7. Fleming, Peter, *Operation SEA LION,* New York: Simon and Schuster, 1957

8. *Fuehrer Directives and Other Top-level Directives of the Wehrmacht,* Washington, D.C., 1948

9. *Germany, Naval Historical, German Staff Planning, World War II,* Washington: Office of Chief of Naval Operations, 1949

10. Hinsley, Francis Harry, *Hitler's Strategy*, Cambridge: The University Press, 1951

11. Joint Pub 1, *Joint Warfare of the Armed Forces of the United States,* Washington: Joint Chiefs of Staff, 2000

12. Joint Pub 3-0, *Doctrine for Joint Operations,* Washington: Joint Chiefs of Staff, 2001

13. Joint Pub 5-0, *Doctrine for Planning Joint Operations,* Washington: Joint Chiefs of Staff, 1995

14. Kecskemeti, Paul, *Strategic Surrender,* Stanford, California: Stanford University Press, 1958

15. Keegan, John, *The Second World War,* London: Penguin Books, 1989

16. Kieser, Egbert, *Hitler on the Doorstep: Operation 'SEA LION' the German Plan to Invade Britain, 1940,* Annapolis: Naval Institute Press, 1997

17. Leach, Barry, *German General Staff, Weapons Book No. 32,* Ed., Mason, David, New York: Ballantine Books, Inc., 1973

18. *Operation SEA LION,* Ed., Cox, Richard, San Rafael: Presidio Press, 1977

19. Overy, Richard, *The Battle of Britain: The Myth and the Reality,* New York: W.W. Norton & Company, 2000

20. Saunders, Commander Malcolm G., "Operation Catapult: Britain Attacks the Vichy Fleet," *History of the Second World War,* Ed. Pitt, Barrie, Marshall Cavendish Corp, 1978

21. "Text of the Nazi-Soviet Pact," On-line. Internet, 27 July 2002, Available from: The History Place, www.historyplace.com/worldwar2/timeline/pact.htm

22. "The Blitz Begins," On-line. Internet, 8 August 2002, Available from: Historical Society Online, www.battleofbritain.net/section-6/blitz-p01.html

23. Von der Porten, Edward, *Pictorial History of the Kriegsmarine in World War II,* New York: Thomas Y. Crowell Company, 1976

24. Wilmont, Chester, *The Struggle for Europe,* New York: Harper & Brothers Publishers, 1952

www.ingramcontent.com/pod-product-compliance
Lightning Source LLC
Chambersburg PA
CBHW081300170426
43198CB00017B/2862